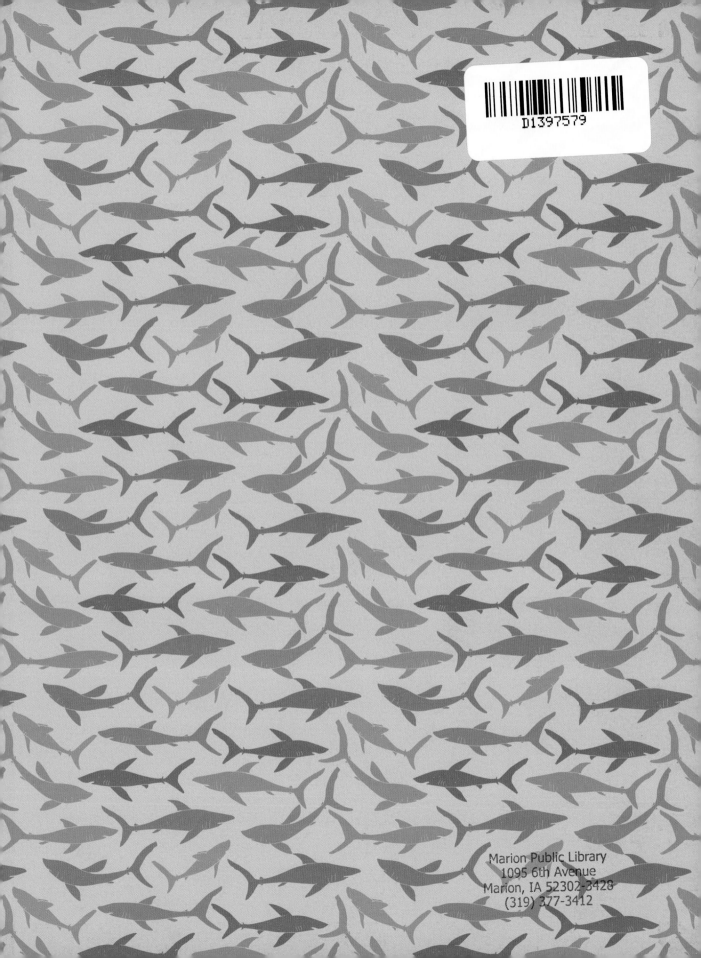

Shark Expedition

SEEKING GIANT SHARKS:
A SHARK DIVER'S QUEST
FOR WHALE SHARKS, BASKING SHARKS,
AND MANTA RAYS

by Mary M. Cerullo
Photographs by Jeffrey L. Rotman

Consultant: James Sulikowski, PhD
Marine Science Department, University of New England

COMPASS POINT BOOKS
a capstone imprint

Compass Point Books are published by Capstone,
1710 Roe Crest Drive, North Mankato, Minnesota 56003
www.capstonepub.com

Editorial Credits
Kristen Mohn, editor; Veronica Scott, designer; Svetlana Zhurkin, media researcher;
Tori Abraham, production specialist

Photo Credits
All photographs by Jeffrey L. Rotman with the exception of:
Asher Gal, 1 (bottom); Isabelle Delafosse, 3, 40 (right); Shutterstock: Olinchuk, 7 (bottom),
ronfromyork, 19, tororo reaction, 16–17, Volina, 24 (right)
Design Elements by Shutterstock

Library of Congress Cataloging-in-Publication Data
Cerullo, Mary M., author.
  Seeking giant sharks : a shark diver's quest for whale sharks, basking sharks, and manta rays / by
Mary M. Cerullo; photographs by Jeffrey L. Rotman.
pages cm. — (Compass point books. Shark expedition)
  Summary: "Provides information on plankton-feeders including whale sharks, basking sharks,
hammerheads, and manta rays, and shares a shark diver's experiences searching for and
photographing them"— Provided by publisher.
  Includes index.
  ISBN 978-0-7565-4885-8 (library binding)
  ISBN 978-0-7565-4908-4 (paperback)
  ISBN 978-0-7565-4912-1 (eBook PDF)
1. Whale shark—Juvenile literature. 2. Basking shark—Juvenile literature. 3. Manta birostris—
Juvenile literature. 4. Rotman, Jeffrey L.—Juvenile literature. 5. Wildlife photography—Juvenile
literature. 6. Underwater photography—Juvenile literature. [1. Manta rays.] I. Rotman, Jeffrey L.,
illustrator. II. Title.
  QL638.95.R4C42 2015
  597.3—dc23   2014008991

To Arthur, Still the One—MMC
For Wayne, thanks for teaching an old dog new tricks—JLR

Printed in the United States of America in
North Mankato, Minnesota
032014   008087CGF14

TABLE OF CONTENTS

THE LARGEST OF THEM ALL
WHALE SHARKS

If you know just one thing about whale sharks, it's probably this: The whale shark is the biggest fish in the world, but it eats some of the smallest animals in the ocean.

But did you know that the huge beast is perhaps the gentlest shark of all? At least that's what underwater photographer Jeff Rotman says. He calls the whale shark the friendliest shark in the sea.

In the ocean BIG doesn't always mean SCARY. (Of course, sometimes it does.)

A whale shark plays with a golden trevally fish on Ningaloo Reef in Australia.

Jeff has been fascinated with sharks for years. From the tiny pygmy shark to the granddaddy of them all—the whale shark—Jeff loves discovering new things about sharks, rays, and other shark relatives.

WHALE SHARK STATS

AVERAGE LENGTH
32 feet (9.8 meters)

MAXIMUM LENGTH
45 feet (13.7 m)— like most sharks, females are larger than males

MAXIMUM WEIGHT
more than 15 tons (13.6 metric tons)

RANGE
worldwide in temperate and tropical seas

LIFE SPAN
100 years or more

DIET
plankton, krill, squid, and small fish

"What impresses me most about the incredible variety of sharks is how well each species is adapted to live in different parts of the world's oceans and feed on so many different kinds of prey," says Jeff. "The biggest sharks defy the popular image of sharks as fearsome predators with row upon row of sharp teeth. Whale sharks, basking sharks, and manta rays are not at all aggressive, despite the fact that they are the biggest fishes in the ocean."

AUSTRALIA IS A GREAT PLACE TO DINE

Diver Rodney Fox is Australia's most outspoken defender of sharks. He was the one who first introduced Jeff to great whites. Rodney saw that Jeff shared his passion for sharks, so he invited him to meet the whale sharks of Australia's Ningaloo Reef.

April and May are a perfect time to spot whale sharks there. Cold currents rise up from the deep ocean off the west coast of Australia. They provide the fertilizer that makes tiny plants called phytoplankton bloom. Phytoplankton feed swarms of tiny animals called zooplankton, which in turn feed larger animals, such as squid and small fish. Any of these could soon find themselves in the belly of a whale shark. And, if lucky, a shark photographer could find himself or herself with a great close-up of the biggest shark in the world.

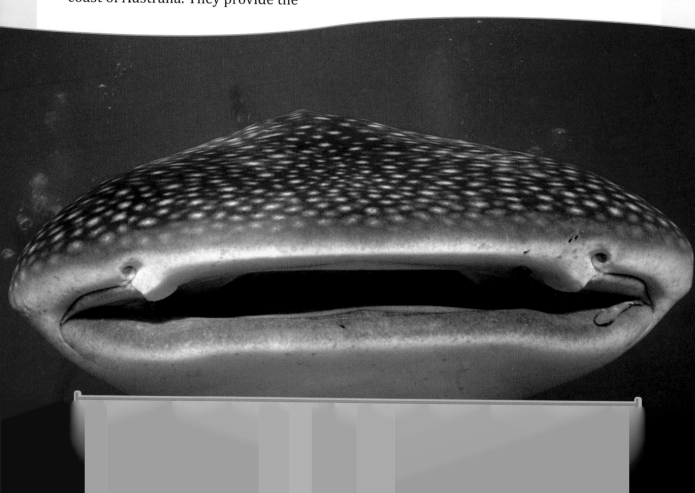

NINGALOO REEF

Ningaloo Reef extends for 160 miles (257 kilometers) along the coast of western Australia. In some places the fringing reef is so close to shore that snorkelers and divers can step off the beach and soon be swimming among hundreds of kinds of colorful reef fish, corals, and shellfish.

hawksbill turtle

In addition to whale sharks, manta rays, humpback whales, dolphins, and dugongs make Ningaloo Marine Park their winter retreat. And mother loggerhead, green, and hawksbill turtles clamber onto its beaches to lay their eggs.

Indian Ocean

AUSTRALIA

NINGALOO

FACT:

It might be terrifying to face a whale shark underwater, but humans have nothing to fear. Scientists don't believe whale sharks use their teeth to bite or chew. And even if you did somehow fall into a whale shark's nearly 5-foot- (1.5-m-) wide mouth, it would simply spit you back out. Plankton and small fish don't have a chance, but humans aren't on a whale shark's menu.

Like basking sharks and the deep-sea megamouth sharks, the whale shark is a filter feeder. It swims forward, mouth wide open, to ram water and food into its gigantic mouth. (Its width is about the height of an average 9-year-old!)

Along with the water come tiny snacks, including fish eggs, shrimp, and krill. The water is flushed back out, but the bits of food are forced up to the roof of the mouth, where they get stuck in a mucous covering. The whale shark gulps, and down go the plankton and other goodies.

A whale shark's waking hours are spent swimming and eating, eating and swimming. But every so often, it stops feeding and does what's best described as a whale shark version of a cough. You wouldn't want to be on the receiving end of that. Scientists think it is how the sharks clean trapped food particles off mouthparts called gill rakers. Wouldn't it be handy to just cough instead of brushing your teeth?

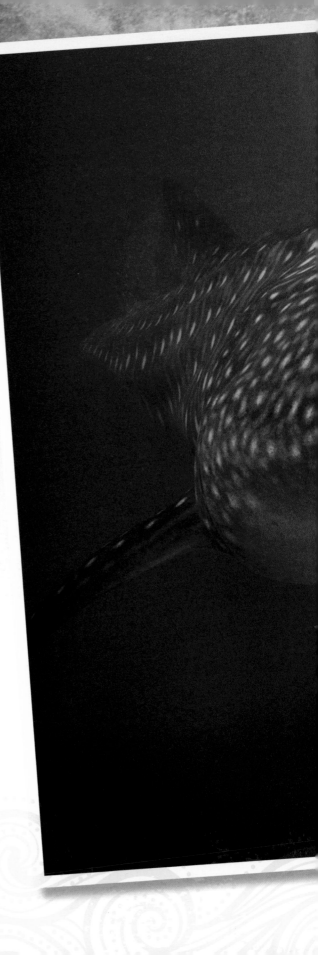

pelagic squid

FACT:

Though primarily filter feeders, whale sharks also capture larger prey such as squid, sardines, and anchovies.

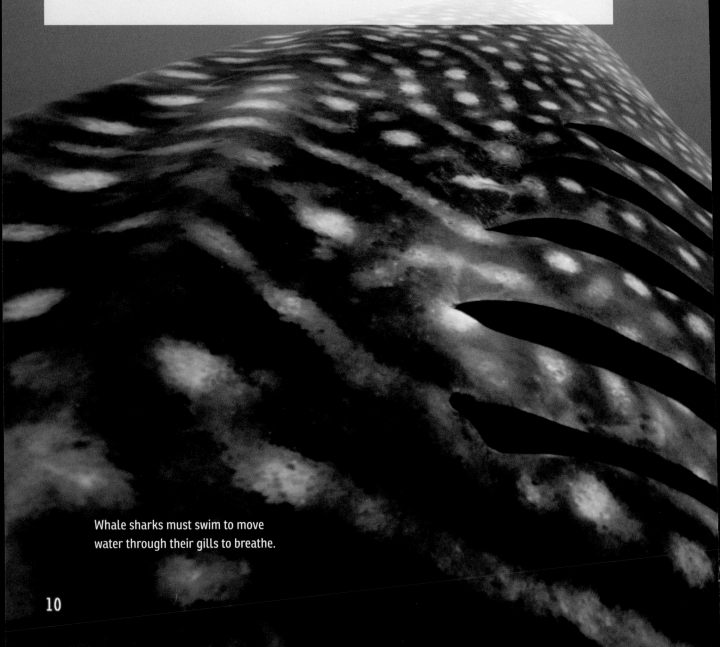

THE HUNT IS ON

Jeff was ready to meet the whale sharks. But he and Rodney Fox needed help to find them. To discover where they were feeding, a spotter plane flew over Ningaloo Reef each day to scout the sharks' location.

On the fourth day of searching, the pilot spotted whale sharks where the coral reef drops off sharply into deep water. He radioed the divers, who then headed their boat toward the action.

Whale sharks must swim to move water through their gills to breathe.

Jeff and Rodney strapped on their gear and tumbled backward off the side of the boat. They peered in the direction the spotter had instructed. Success!

At 20 feet (6 m) below the surface, a ghostly image appeared in the distance. Jeff watched in amazement as an enormous, gaping mouth came steadily toward him. The huge whale shark seemed unaware that Jeff was in its path. Just when it seemed as if it might swallow him up, the shark dipped down and swam under him. Jeff found himself staring down at the giant gray back passing beneath him, beautifully mottled with pale yellow stripes and spots.

WHY DO DIVERS FALL BACKWARD OFF A BOAT?

Beginning divers are usually taught to sit on the rail of a small boat and fall backward into the water as they hold onto their face masks. This way the dive masks stay in place and the heavy dive tanks don't land on top of them. If a diver fell face first into the water, he or she might hit the side of the boat—a tough way to start an underwater adventure. Another option is the giant stride, for a diver who wants to just step off into the blue. But it's called the giant stride for a reason—if you don't jump far enough out, your tank will hit the side of the boat.

Some divers take a giant stride to enter the water.

Jeff had never been close to a whale shark before. "Nothing prepares you to meet an animal of this size underwater," said Jeff. "It's a different kind of 'large' altogether from a great white shark. A great white is the size of a family car. The whale shark is a school bus. Plus, objects underwater look bigger than they actually are, which made it seem humongous!"

Fifteen to 20 remoras swam along beneath the white belly of the whale shark. They know a good thing when they see it. Also called suckerfish, remoras stick to whale sharks using suction cups on their heads, grabbing scraps of food from their host as they are carried along. And who would attack a remora under the shelter of such a huge protector?

Jeff was so intent on capturing photographs that he lost all fear of the huge animal. The whale shark went by him so slowly that he couldn't resist grabbing onto its dorsal fin as it passed. Holding on with one hand, Jeff kept shooting pictures with the other. As he was dragged through the water, he got close-up shots of its mouth, eyes, gills, and the spots that identify each individual whale shark.

Remoras stick to the belly of a whale shark.

FACT:

The whale shark's skin is very thick—4 inches (10 centimeters) or more. Skin this thick can resist the bites of all but great whites and a few other fierce predators. The yellow-white stripes and spots that cover the shark's back help it blend in among shafts of sunlight reaching into the water, giving the enormous fish a bit of camouflage as it hunts.

Jeff's whale shark taxi started to dive very slowly and gently. As he went deeper and deeper, Jeff had to keep swallowing to clear his ears to equalize the pressure. Meanwhile, the whale shark continued its lazy journey downward, sometimes actively swimming, sometimes gliding, in search of food.

After a few minutes, Jeff noticed that the light around him was fading. He looked at his depth gauge. He was 130 feet (39.6 m) below the surface. But still he held onto the fin. Then, as if it was getting tired of its hitchhiker, the whale shark sped up and began to dive more steeply. Finally, Jeff had to let go.

It was only then that he realized he was running out of air and that his ears were aching from the intense pressure. He kicked for the surface as quickly as he could, but he had to stop often to give his body time to adjust to the changing water pressure.

THE BENDS

Why couldn't Jeff just rocket for the surface as fast as possible? He had to make sure that he didn't get a very serious condition that doctors call decompression sickness and divers call the bends.

Think of what happens when you unscrew the cap on a bottle of soda. The gas that was dissolved in the liquid at high pressure comes out as bubbles when the pressure is released.

Scuba divers breathe compressed gases from their air tanks. If a diver rises too quickly, bubbles of gas can form in the bloodstream and move around the body, especially to shoulders, elbows, knees, and ankles. The bubbles can cause intense pain and potentially even death.

"My amazement at this gentle giant made it easy to forget my number one safety rule: Never get too comfortable around a shark." says Jeff. "Had the shark decided to give me a slap with its enormous tail, it would have knocked me into the next ocean— or at least unconscious!"

A HOME FOR WHALE SHARKS

Whale sharks can grow to be about 45 feet (13.7 m) long. Their size makes them way too big to be kept in most aquariums. One place that has been able to house whale sharks is the Churaumi Aquarium in Okinawa, Japan. Several whale sharks swim with manta rays, yellowfin tuna, and other big fish inside a tank that holds nearly 2 million gallons (7,500 cubic meters) of seawater. That's enough water to fill about 50,000 bathtubs.

In the ocean you may find whale sharks in tropical seas, like those around Australia, as well as in the warm waters off Mexico and Asia. At one time there was a market for whale shark meat in Asia. Today whale sharks are protected from fishing.

SHY SHARK
BASKING SHARKS

A whale shark is curious and approachable. A basking shark—another giant—is the exact opposite. Perhaps it comes from living in cold, murky water, where it barely can see any of its neighbors through the gloom. This giant shark is used to traveling alone or in small groups. It does not seem to welcome human companions like Jeff who want to swim alongside it.

The basking shark plows through the water with its mouth open, catching zooplankton and small fish on its gill rakers. Filter feeding must work well for it, because a basking shark can grow to about 33 feet (10 m), making it the world's second largest fish after the whale shark.

A basking shark opens its mouth wide to catch plankton.

The first time Jeff tried to get close enough to a basking shark to take its picture was one summer in the Irish Sea. In July huge blooms of phytoplankton turn the waters off the Isle of Man into a pea-green sea soup. "The water here between Scotland and Wales is freezing cold, even in summer, and the weather is always rainy and foggy," Jeff recalled. But that makes it a perfect spot to look for basking sharks.

SCOTLAND

ISLE OF MAN

NORTHERN
IRELAND

IRELAND

ENGLAND

WALES

BASKING SHARK STATS

AVERAGE LENGTH
22 feet (6.7 m)

RANGE
temperate coastal waters

MAXIMUM LENGTH
33 feet (10 m)

LIFE SPAN
50 years

MAXIMUM WEIGHT
4 tons (3.6 metric tons)

DIET
plankton, krill, and jellyfish

Scientists estimate that a large
basking shark can filter nearly
400,000 gallons (1,500 cubic meters)
of water per hour.

HIDE AND SEEK

Day after day Jeff waited and watched, hoping to see a giant dorsal fin peek above the water. The basking shark likely got its name from its habit of cruising near the surface. To early shark watchers, it may have appeared that the sharks were basking in the sun like sunbathers. But they were most likely feeding on plankton, which tend to drift on ocean currents near the surface.

That behavior made basking sharks easy for fishermen to catch. They were almost hunted to extinction, but now basking sharks and whale sharks are protected by international agreement.

Jeff knew that basking sharks are shy and easily frightened. He also knew that the bubbles and the gurgling sounds from a scuba tank could scare them away, so he had to plan his dives carefully. To be as quiet as possible, he used a mask and snorkel instead of a tank, which meant he would have to hold his breath for as long as he could. "We even put Vaseline on the rubber straps of our flippers so they wouldn't squeak against our heels," he said, "because as soon as the shark senses that you are there, it disappears."

The basking sharks would flee if they heard a boat engine. Instead the divers quietly rowed an inflatable rubber raft out to the area where the basking sharks fed. When they got close, Jeff slipped silently into the water. He took a big gulp of air and dove down into the cold, gray-green water. The plankton was so thick he couldn't see very far in any direction.

In fact, the water was so murky and the light so dim that Jeff didn't see the basking shark at all—until it was right on top of him. Startled, Jeff snapped as many photographs as he could before the animal retreated into the gloom like a ghost disappearing into the mist.

IF AT FIRST YOU DON'T SUCCEED ...

Not every expedition is a success. "I spent two weeks trying to get a good photograph," Jeff said. "Unfortunately, I wasn't happy with any of my pictures. So I returned the next year—on my honeymoon!"

It might not have been the type of honeymoon that anyone but a diver would dream of, but after two more weeks on the Isle of Man, Jeff finally got the photos he wanted.

BLUE WATER SURPRISE
GIANT MANTA RAYS

Did you ever discover something you never expected to find that was even better than what you were actually looking for? That's what happened to Jeff during an expedition with divers hunting supersized swordfish and tuna.

Jeff met up with the group, called Blue Water Hunters, in the Socorro Islands, about 250 miles (400 km) south of Mexico's Baja California. Each member of the group is a champion free diving underwater hunter. They spend more than eight hours a day in the water, diving down 80 to 100 feet (24 to 30 m) without scuba gear, for a chance to catch a giant "trophy" fish using only a spear gun.

The diving group did find some really big fish on that expedition, but not the ones they were expecting. Instead they found what a scientist has described as "small cars with wings."

A Blue Water Hunter catches a giant wahoo, one of the fastest fish in the ocean.

UNITED STATES

MEXICO

SOCORRO ISLANDS

Some giant mantas have a "wingspan" of nearly 30 feet (9 m).

Jeff's plan was to take photographs of the Blue Water Hunters swimming in the open sea. "A Blue Water Hunter is the closest thing to a man-fish," Jeff says. They have trained themselves to slow their heart rates so that they can hold their breath for minutes at a time.

Their boat steamed out to an area of the Pacific Ocean that was a deep, dark blue, a sign that the water there was thousands of feet deep. The hunters jumped overboard as gleefully as kids diving into a swimming pool.

Even though Jeff is an expert diver, he admitted that diving in the open ocean with miles of water beneath you can be a bit scary. But in he went with the Blue Water Hunters.

Jeff was shooting photographs of the hunters as they made dive after dive, when suddenly one, then two, then six giant manta rays swarmed around them. The hunters forgot their quest for giant tuna and wahoo. They swam back to the boat to trade their spear guns for underwater cameras.

GIANT MANTA RAY STATS

AVERAGE WIDTH
17 to 22 feet (5 to 6.7 m)

MAXIMUM WIDTH
29.5 feet (9 m)

MAXIMUM WEIGHT
about 3 tons (2.7 metric tons)

RANGE
tropical and temperate oceans

LIFE SPAN
up to 40 years

DIET
plankton, krill, and jellyfish

NICKNAME
devilfish

A MOST UNUSUAL SKELETON

Rays and sharks are close relatives. Unlike most other fish, which have hard, bony skeletons like ours, sharks and rays have skeletons made of cartilage. That is the same flexible material you have in your ears and the tip of your nose. Cartilage in the fins of the manta ray gives it the flexibility and support it needs to "fly" gracefully through the water.

The noodlelike strands of cartilage are also what make sharks so highly prized for use in shark fin soup. Each year about 40 million sharks are caught just for their fins.

A giant ray gives a ride to a
remora—and to the diver
holding onto the remora's tail.

Remoras attach themselves to giant
rays as well as whale sharks and others,
seeking protection and free food.

Forgetting about their fishing trip, the hunters played with the mantas for hours each day. Often the rays would roll over like puppies. Black splotches on their white bellies helped the divers identify individual rays. Remoras hitchhiked anywhere they could attach themselves to the giant fish.

Sometimes a manta ray would float just a few feet above the head of a diver, so close that the diver could have reached up and scratched its belly. Some scientists think this is the same behavior that the manta rays display at cleaning stations. Perhaps the rays thought the divers were there to clean them.

AT THE CAR WASH

Cleaning stations are where sea animals gather to have small cleaner fish pick off parasites that irritate their skin, mouth, and gills. When a manta ray stops and hovers like a helicopter, it is a signal to the cleaner that the ray is not planning to eat it. It's waiting its turn to be cleaned. After the cleaners nibble parasites off the ray's body, they may turn their attention to the remoras that accompany the manta and help them out as well.

Blue Water Hunter Terry Maas hitches
a ride on a giant manta ray.

THE DEVILFISH ROLLER COASTER

That day at the Socorro Islands, champion American free diver Terry Maas dove to about 35 feet (10.7 m). There a manta ray came up to Terry, slowed down, and looked right at him. Terry saw it as an invitation. He grabbed onto the manta ray's scaly head and draped himself across the big fish's back. Terry got the ride of his life.

The manta ray gently flapped its "wings," which are overgrown pectoral fins. The ray made graceful loops, like a slow-motion roller coaster. After about three minutes, Terry had to return to the surface to take a breath. When he dove back down, the manta ray was waiting for him. Again and again, the ride continued after Terry returned from gulping a lungful of air. It was as if the manta ray was a taxi waiting for its passenger.

Manta rays don't have stingers on their tails like their stingray relatives.

A manta ray has small fins that resemble horns on either side of its head to herd zooplankton, such as copepods, shrimp, and newly hatched fish, into its mouth. The fins started out as side fins. While the baby manta ray was still growing inside its mother, pieces of the side fins separated to become head fins. (Scientists call them cephalic fins.) When it is swimming fast, a manta ray can curl up the fins to make itself more streamlined.

The helpful fins may be the reason that the manta ray was once called devilfish—they reminded people of a devil's horns. Another legend that may have made people fearful of manta rays was based on their ability to leap out of the water. Some tales claim that mantas would jump onto small boats to crush sailors. (It may have happened—by accident.) It is more likely that mantas breach like whales to scrape parasites off their skin as they slap the water coming back down.

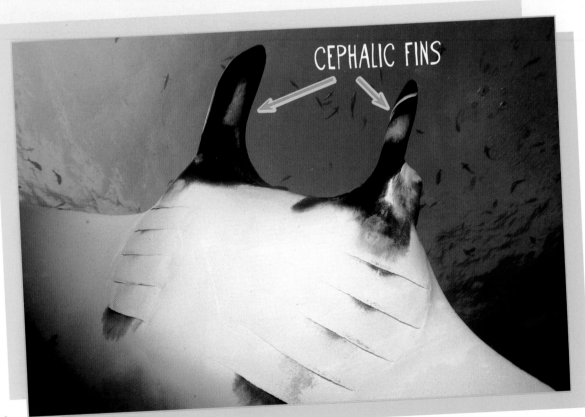

CEPHALIC FINS

THE FUTURE FOR GIANTS

Some mantas are accidentally caught in fishing nets. Others are hunted outright. Jeff believes manta rays need to be better protected from humans who pursue them.

Many manta rays are caught for food and for their gills, which are used to make Asian medicines. Patients are told that the gills of these fish filter out particles from seawater, so the gills should help filter out diseases or poisons from the human body.

But there is no scientific evidence that this is true.

Guy Stevens, founder and director of the Manta Trust, helped convince representatives from 178 countries to vote to protect mantas. Mantas were added to a list of protected plants and animals under international rules in March 2013. This action can help control the trade in manta ray gills.

a manta ray caught in a fishing net

Giant fish like the whale shark are now protected by international agreement.

Guy says that there is another important thing that may help protect manta rays—us! Tourists such as scuba divers and snorkelers spend more than $140 million a year to visit tropical waters in Mexico, Fiji, Indonesia, Sri Lanka, and India, where mantas and tourists can swim together. Some of that money goes to programs that help protect ocean habitats and preserve them for the future.

Whale sharks, basking sharks, and manta rays are listed as protected animals by CITES—the Convention on International Trade in Endangered Species. It is proof that the world is beginning to appreciate the gentle giants and their place in the sea.

GLOSSARY

breach—to leap partly or completely out of the water, a behavior usually seen in humpback whales and dolphins

cartilage—a strong, rubbery tissue that connects bones in people and animals; in sharks, the entire skeleton is composed of cartilage rather than bone

cephalic fin—one of two small fins on either side of a manta ray's head, which channel food toward its mouth; head fin

cleaner fish—a small fish, often with a distinctive stripe that identifies it as an animal that picks off parasites and dead skin from larger fish

cleaning station—an area in the ocean where fish gather to be cleaned of parasites

copepod—a shrimplike zooplankton that is a key animal in ocean food webs

dorsal fin—a back fin, which helps to keep a fish upright in the water

dugong—a relative of a manatee, which lives along the coastlines of the Indian and Pacific oceans

extinction—the state that results when a species has died out completely

filter feeder—a marine animal that strains plankton out of the water

fringing reef—a coral reef that grows close to shore

gill rakers—comblike bristles that keep food particles from clogging a shark's gills

pectoral fins—side fins, which fish use for turning and stopping

phytoplankton—one-celled, drifting aquatic plants that float with the waves and currents

reef—a formation on the ocean floor composed of the skeletons of coral animals, living and dead, as well as sea urchin spines, seashells, worm casings, seaweed, and sponges

remora—a fish with a suction disk on the top of its head with which it attaches itself to sharks, turtles, or other larger animals; it often eats scraps from its host's meals

wahoo—a prized game fish known for its tasty flesh; it can swim up to 60 miles per hour (97 kph) and may weigh up to 183 pounds (83 kg)

zooplankton—floating animals, including microscopic animals as well as the larval stages of many sea creatures such as crabs, sea stars, and fish

READ MORE

Cerullo, Mary M. *Giant Squid: Searching for a Sea Monster.*
Smithsonian. North Mankato, Minn.: Capstone Press, 2012.

Discovery Channel. *The Big Book of Sharks.*
New York: Time Home Entertainment, 2012.

Musgrave, Ruth. *National Geographic Kids Everything Sharks.*
Washington, D.C.: National Geographic, 2011.

INTERNET SITES

Use FactHound to find Internet sites related to this book.
All of the sites on FactHound have been researched by our staff.

Here's all you do:

Visit *www.facthound.com*

Type in this code:
9780756548858

AUTHOR

Mary M. Cerullo has been teaching and writing about the ocean and natural history for 40 years. She has written more than 20 children's books on ocean life. Mary is also associate director of the conservation organization Friends of Casco Bay/Casco Baykeeper in Maine, where she lives with her family.

Mary with granddaughter Taylor

PHOTOGRAPHER

Jeffrey L. Rotman is one of the world's leading underwater photographers. Diving and shooting for more than 40 years—and in nearly every ocean and sea in the world—this Boston native combines an artist's eye with a naturalist's knowledge of his subjects. His photography has been featured on television and in print worldwide. Jeff and his family live in New Jersey.

Jeff with sons Matthew and Thomas

INDEX

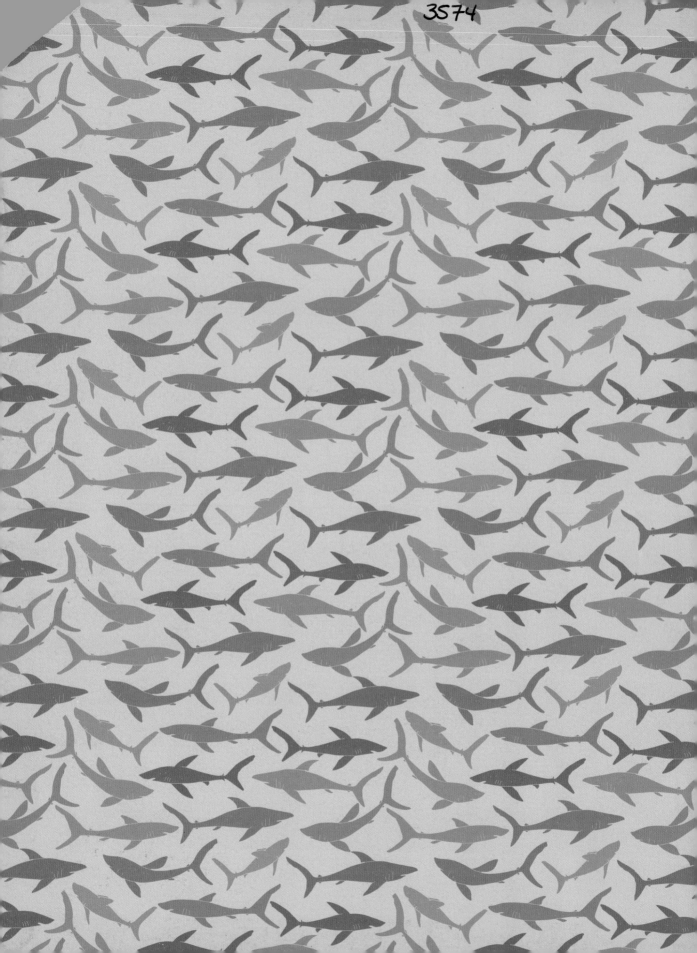

3574